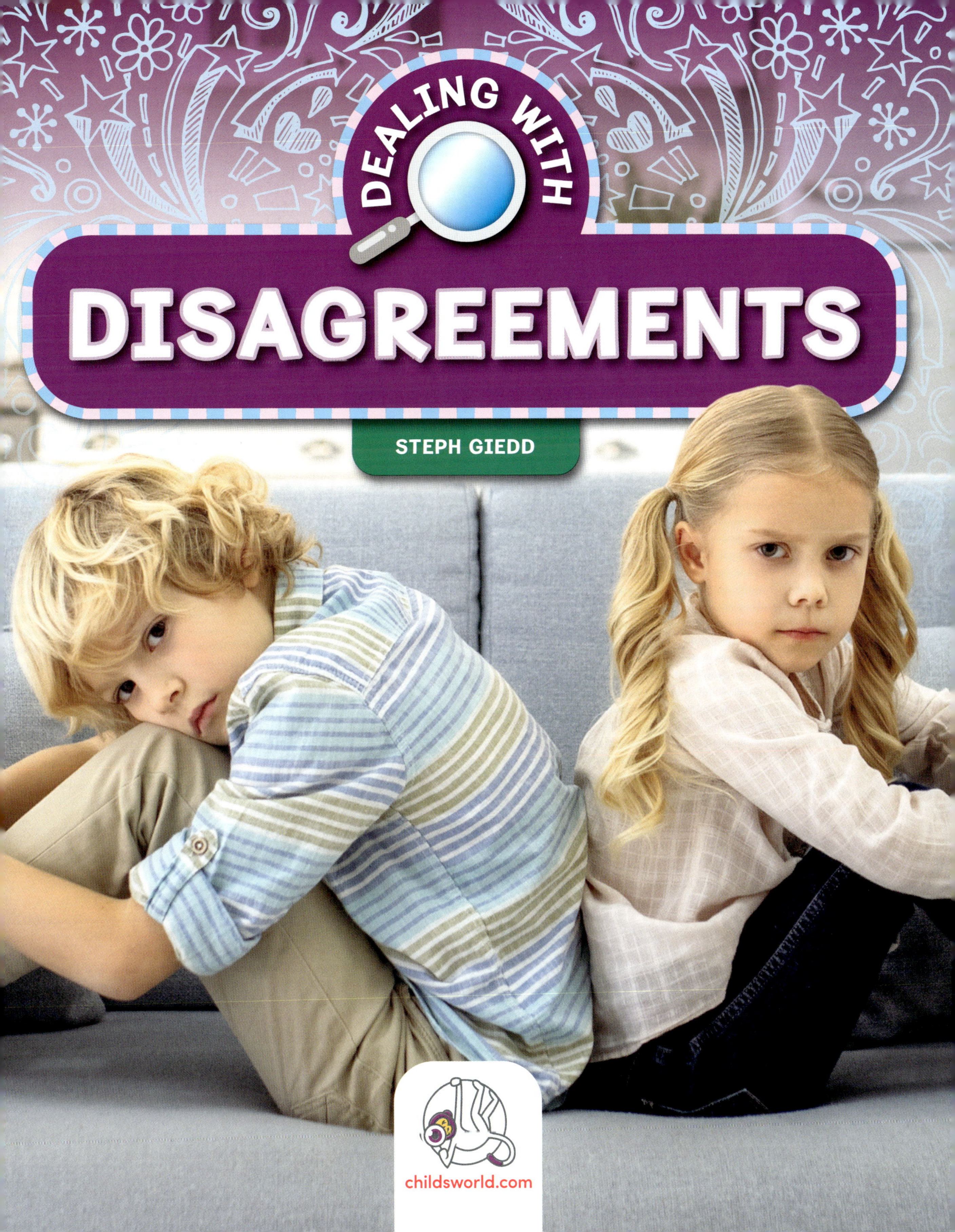
DEALING WITH
DISAGREEMENTS
STEPH GIEDD
childsworld.com

Published by The Child's World®
800-599-READ • www.childsworld.com

Photography Credits
Photographs ©: iStockphoto, cover, 1, 18–19; Shutterstock Images, 5, 6–7, 11, 17, 22; G Point Studio/iStockphoto, 8; Wavebreak Media/Shutterstock Images, 14; Dikushin Dmitry/Shutterstock Images, 20

ISBN Information
9781503885424 (Reinforced Library Binding)
9781503885578 (Portable Document Format)
9781503886216 (Online Multi-user eBook)
9781503886858 (Electronic Publication)

LCCN 2023937456

Printed in the United States of America

Steph Giedd is a former high school English teacher who now works as an editor. Originally from southern Iowa, Giedd lives in Minneapolis, Minnesota, with her husband, daughter, and pets.

TABLE OF CONTENTS

When Disagreements Happen

Sometimes people disagree about things. They may disagree on how to play a game, or whose turn it is. They may disagree on who gets the last cookie. No matter how big or small the problem is, disagreements can cause fights. It is important to deal with disagreements. Working out problems keeps relationships strong. If problems do not get solved, disagreements can hurt friendships.

Even people who love each other disagree sometimes.

Children may disagree with adults. For example, a parent might say that 9:00 p.m. is a good bedtime. But a kid may think he or she should stay up until 10:00 p.m. Or a parent may say that it is important to eat vegetables. But the child doesn't like them. Or maybe a teacher says it is another child's turn on the swing. But the child isn't ready to share.

Sharing is one way to make new friends.

People can respect each other even when they have different opinions.

When kids disagree with a friend or an adult, it can cause a lot of strong feelings. They may feel angry or sad. They may feel embarrassed if they are wrong. They may feel pride if they are right. Kids need to know how to handle these strong feelings. If they do not deal with their feelings, those **emotions** may cause fights, hurt relationships, and start more disagreements. Learning how to disagree respectfully is an important life skill.

Coping with Disagreements

People can become emotional when disagreements happen. This is especially true if the disagreement is about something they really care about. Sometimes these strong emotions can be unhelpful. People can have a hard time thinking clearly when they are angry. This can also make it harder to solve the problem. **Conflicts** are easier to fix if everyone is calm. It is important for people to deal with their strong emotions during a disagreement.

Interrupting others during a disagreement can make them feel like their opinions are not important.

This can be hard, but there are ways to make it easier.

First, it is important for the people involved in a disagreement to try to calm down. They can take a deep breath. This can help their bodies and minds relax. They should take a moment to think about what they want to say. After gathering their thoughts and calming down, people should explain their feelings. It's important to be respectful and not place blame while sharing feelings.

People can share their feelings by using "I" statements to avoid placing blame. For example, saying, "You are not listening to me" places blame. This can make the other person feel **defensive**. Saying, "I feel like my opinion isn't being heard" shares the concern without placing blame.

Let's Use "I" Statements

Using "I" statements is a good way for people to express their feelings calmly and respectfully.

Instead of...	Try...
You are mean!	I felt sad when you said I was annoying.
You never let me pick!	I would really like to choose the movie today.
You did not do your chores!	I feel frustrated when I have to do the chores by myself.
You need to share!	I would like to play with you.

Sometimes doing something active can help people feel less angry.

Pros and Cons

Sometimes making a pros and cons list can help settle a disagreement. To make a pros and cons list, people write down the positive things and the negative things about each option. This can help people decide which option is better.

Next, each person should try to think of some positive, fair **solutions**. Choose a solution that everyone can agree with. People may have to **compromise**. If the problem seems too difficult to solve, they can ask an adult for help.

Sometimes a problem can be so frustrating that people start insulting each other. Sometimes people may even start **physically** hurting each other. No matter how mad someone gets, doing these things only makes the situation worse. Hurting someone is never OK, even if someone else starts doing it first. If a disagreement gets **violent**, people should leave the situation and find a trusted adult.

Helping a Friend Deal with Disagreements

Friends can help each other solve problems. If a friend is having a disagreement with someone, it can help to talk about it with someone not involved in the conflict. Friends can also help each other think of solutions.

Encourage friends to be fair and to express their feelings without anger. Sometimes a person may not understand a friend's feelings. That is why it is important to talk about feelings and think about how others might be feeling.

If a disagreement seems too hard to handle alone, it is always OK to ask an adult for help.

Sometimes a friend with a problem may not want to talk or think about it anymore. The friend might want to do something fun to help them calm down. Going for a walk or doing something enjoyable like playing a game together may be just what the friend needs.

If a friend is having trouble controlling his or her emotions, try to understand the friend's feelings. But encourage the friend to avoid saying mean things about the person the friend is disagreeing with. Trying to help the friend see the problem from the other person's point of view can be helpful, too.

People in a conflict can each take turns speaking so that they all get a chance to share their feelings.

When people get upset, taking a break and calming down can stop them from saying hurtful things.

It is important to try to be fair when looking for a solution. When thinking of solutions, what's something that helps everyone win? Or at least, what seems fair? If there does not seem to be a fair solution, or if someone will not calm down, walking away is an OK option, too. Walking away allows everyone to calm down and think about solutions.

Wonder More

Wondering about New Information

How much did you know about disagreements before reading this book? What new information did you learn? Write down three new facts that this book taught you. Was the new information surprising? Why or why not?

Wondering How It Matters

What is one disagreement you have had recently? How did it make you feel? If you cannot think of a personal connection, imagine disagreements that other kids might have. What impact might disagreements have on their lives?

Wondering Why

Why do you think it's important to learn about how to deal with disagreements? How might learning about this topic help you?

Ways to Keep Wondering

Dealing with disagreements is a complex topic. After reading this book, what questions do you have about dealing with disagreements? What can you do to learn more about this topic?

Fast Facts

- People can disagree about a lot of things.
- Disagreements can cause emotions such as anger, embarrassment, and frustration.
- Learning how to solve conflicts is important for relationships.
- It's important for people to be respectful to each other, even when they disagree about something.
- Insults, name-calling, and physical fighting only make problems worse.
- People can express feelings using "I" statements.
- When considering solutions to a problem, it's important to think about what's fair for everyone.

Glossary

compromise (KOM-pruh-mize) When people compromise, they accept a solution that includes parts of what they both want. People can compromise to solve disagreements.

conflicts (KON-fliktz) Conflicts are problems or disagreements. It is important to stay respectful during conflicts.

defensive (deh-FEN-siv) When people are defensive, they get upset when someone tells them they are wrong. It can be hard to solve disagreements when someone is defensive.

emotions (ee-MOH-shuns) Emotions are feelings, such as sadness, fear, or joy. Disagreements can cause strong emotions.

physically (FIZ-ik-lee) When people hurt someone physically, they hurt the person's body. It is not OK to physically hurt someone.

solutions (suh-LOO-shuns) Solutions are answers to problems. Friends can work together to brainstorm solutions to disagreements.

violent (VY-uh-lent) Violent conflicts are conflicts where people physically hurt each other. If a conflict becomes violent, it is important to leave and find a trusted adult.

Find Out More

In the Library

An, Priscilla. *Mindfulness on the Playground.* Parker, CO: The Child's World, 2024.

Huebner, Dawn. *The Sibling Survival Guide: Surefire Ways to Solve Conflicts, Reduce Rivalry, and Have More Fun with Your Brothers and Sisters.* Philadelphia, PA: Jessica Kingsley Publishers, 2021.

Kennedy-Moore, Eileen, and Christine McLaughlin. *Growing Friendships: A Kid's Guide to Making and Keeping Friends.* Hillsboro, OR: Beyond Words, 2017.

On the Web

Visit our website for links about dealing with disagreements:
childsworld.com/links

Note to Parents, Caregivers, Teachers, and Librarians: We routinely verify our Web links to make sure they are safe and active sites. So encourage your readers to check them out!

Index